Waiting in Joyful Hope

Dail
Adve

Michelle Francl-Donnay

LITURGICAL PRESS

Collegeville, Minnesota

www.litpress.org

Nihil Obstat: Reverend Robert Harren, J.C.L., *Censor deputatus.*
Imprimatur: ✠ Most Reverend Donald J. Kettler, J.C.L., Bishop of
Saint Cloud, March 18, 2020.

Cover design by Monica Bokinskie. Cover art courtesy of Getty
Images.

Daily Scripture excerpts in this work are from the *Lectionary for Mass
for Use in the Dioceses of the United States of America, second typical
edition* © 2001, 1998, 1997, 1986, 1970 Confraternity of Christian
Doctrine, Inc., Washington, DC. Used with permission. All rights
reserved. No portion of this text may be reproduced by any means
without permission in writing from the copyright owner.

Other Scripture texts in this work are taken from the *New American
Bible, revised edition* © 2010, 1991, 1986, 1970 Confraternity of Christian Doctrine, Washington, DC, and are used by permission of the
copyright owner. All Rights Reserved. No part of the New American
Bible may be reproduced in any form without permission in writing
from the copyright owner.

Where noted, excerpt from THE NEW JERUSALEM BIBLE, published and copyright © 1985 by Darton, Longman and Todd Ltd and
Doubleday, a division of Random House, Inc.

ISSN: 1550-803X
ISBN: 978-0-8146-6513-8   978-0-8146-6538-1 (ebook)

Introduction

Come down, begged Isaiah, that the mountains might quake and the nations tremble. As fire makes water swell and seethe, so will your wondrous deeds be known across the earth, promises the prophet (Isa 63:19b-64:1a). I stand in my dark kitchen, watching the water in the glass kettle swell and seethe as it comes to a boil, and contemplate Isaiah's images. Bubbles tumble about, irrepressible, ever changing, refracting the blue light of the flame until the water seems to glow of its own accord.

For all that I yearn for a season filled with quiet and prayerful moments to spend preparing for God's coming, it is not to be. Like the water in the kettle, my Advents seethe, boiling over with things to be done and people to be seen. Yet despite the end-of-year chaos—or perhaps because of it—the rich images in the Advent Scriptures dance irrepressibly through my days. They spill forth light, shining beacons in the drear days. They draw me deeply into the super-luminous darkness where God dwells.

I find in Advent not so much a refuge from the demands of my life and of the world as a series of mysterious contradictions that leave me slightly off balance. The Scriptures of this season promise us light in the midst of the darkness, but they also make clear the demands the kindling of such a light place upon us. They disrupt my preconceptions about what it means that God has come to dwell among us, forcing me to come face-to-face with what it means for me, here and now, to encounter God in human form. These readings put flesh on hope.

In his General Audience last Advent, Pope Francis spoke of the manger as an invitation to contemplation, a reminder of the importance of stopping. Contemplation is sometimes called the art of stealing time. I hope that you can manage to steal a few moments each day this Advent and Christmas season to listen to God's irrepressible, radiant Word, so that its fire might re-kindle a flame in your heart.

For all that Advent propels us toward Christmas, the stable in Bethlehem is not a destination. It is a way station, a momentary gathering of those who will be dispatched to all corners of the earth. Strangers and shepherds and angels stop and then depart as quickly as they came. Not to follow the same paths they came by but to be sent out on new roads and to new lives. May our lives, too, be open to being astonished by what God has done and is doing in the world. And may we always be a people working in joyful hope for the coming of God's kingdom.

FIRST WEEK OF ADVENT

November 29: First Sunday of Advent

Tear Open the Heavens

Readings: Isa 63:16b-17, 19b; 64:2-7; 1 Cor 1:3-9; Mark 13:33-37

Scripture:
Oh, that you would rend the heavens and come down,
   with the mountains quaking before you,
while you wrought awesome deeds we could not hope for.
   (Isa 63:19b; 64:2)

Reflection: I cannot think of Advent without thinking of Alfred Delp, SJ, who in 1944 spent the Advent and Christmas seasons in prison. Delp's writings, letters, and reflections on Advent were smuggled out from prison on scraps of paper by two friends. In one letter, he wrote that he thought it would be a beautiful Christmas. How, you might wonder? Delp was handcuffed night and day and confined to a small cell, facing a death sentence. There would be no moving liturgies, no exquisite manger scenes. But with all the ornaments and romantic imagery stripped away, Delp said he could see clearly the shaking reality of what Christmas promised: God in the flesh, God taking a stand with us against the unimaginable darkness. Christmas, offered Delp, is the chance to celebrate the mystery of the great howling hunger of humankind for God—if we are willing to give over our complacency and pretensions.

In Advent's dark and cold days I am, I confess, often drawn to meditate on the gentle mysteries of a babe wrapped and warm, puffy sheep in the fields and angels in the sky trailing glory. Wondrous stars. Enigmatic strangers from the East. Gold and rare spices. It is the proper and cherished stuff of Christmas pageants. Yet this isn't quite what the people of God asked for through Isaiah. We begged God to tear open the heavens and come down, we pleaded with God to be what we don't dare hope for.

Dare we join with Isaiah and cry out to the heavens this Advent, imploring God to do for us what we cannot bring ourselves to hope for? Might the hungry be fed, might the migrant find safe harbor, might God visit peace on the nations? Shine forth from your cherubim throne, O Lord. Rouse your power and rend the heavens. Come and save us!

Meditation: Delp wrote that to live in the knowledge that the Divine and the human have collided in time requires a willingness to let our romantic notions be burned off, that we might have a clear vision of what is and could be. As Advent lays before us, what do you desire most from God this season, the one thing you dare not hope for?

Prayer: Lord, you loved us enough to tear open the heavens and come to our aid. Rouse your power and come again, show us your face that we might be saved. May we have the patience to wait and the courage to hope.

November 30: Saint Andrew, Apostle

Reaching to the Ends of the Earth

Readings: Rom 10:9-18; Matt 4:18-22

Scripture:
Their voice has gone forth to all the earth,
and their words to the ends of the world. (Rom 10:18b)

Reflection: When I was a young professor it was customary to write to other scientists and ask for a copy of their recent work that you wished to read. Whenever I published a new scientific paper, postcards from all over the world would appear in my mailbox, asking that I send them a copy. Some requests came from places I could not imagine going: from universities in Cuba and the Soviet Union. My words had seemingly gone out to the ends of the earth. Now we can reach the ends of the earth and beyond with a few taps on our phone, our words visible even to astronauts on the International Space Station.

St. Andrew and his fellow apostles were sent out by Jesus to proclaim the good news, to be a voice for the Gospel even to the ends of the earth. But this is not just a job for the apostles and their successors. In his apostolic exhortation *Evangelii Gaudium*, Pope Francis firmly reminds us that we are all, by virtue of our baptism, called to be evangelists, disciples on a mission to all the world. All of us are to raise our voices, living and proclaiming the joy of the Gospel. Do not think that you need special training or must wait to be invited, Pope Francis advises. We can rely on the grace of the Holy Spirit to guide us as well as the gifts the Spirit brings to us: of wisdom and strength and understanding. We must allow the deep joy that comes with our faith to bubble up in every encounter, whether we are whispering words of encouragement to a friend in distress or tweeting the latest news to the ends of the world. Go forth and proclaim the Good News!

Meditation: Preach the Gospel at all times, use words if necessary, advised St. Francis of Assisi. In what ways is the joy of the good news, that God has come to earth and lives among us, visible in your life? How is God calling you to be an evangelist?

Prayer: You are the Word made flesh, O Lord, that speaks to us of joy and of mercy. Help us proclaim you to all the world, in our every action as in our every word.

December 1: Tuesday of the First Week of Advent

Breathing Space

Readings: Isa 11:1-10; Luke 10:21-24

Scripture:
The Spirit of the LORD shall rest upon him:
  a Spirit of wisdom and of understanding,
A Spirit of counsel and of strength . . . (Isa 11:2a)

Reflection: Breathe. I say it to students who are anxious about their work. I say it to colleagues who are teetering on the edge of exasperation—or exhaustion. And at this time of year, as the stack of papers to grade grows and end of semester meetings and holiday events start to elbow each other on my calendar like squirming six-year-olds, I find myself murmuring it to myself over and over again. Breathe. Breathe. Remember to breathe.

The Hebrew word *rúah*, often rendered Spirit in this passage from Isaiah, can also mean wind or breath, and I long in these Advent days for a moment's breathing space. I ache for a touch of the Spirit's strength and wise counsel to waft past my office, taking with it the dust of exhaustion and frustration.

In his conference on perfection, the fifth-century monk and theologian St. John Cassian offered a stronger translation of this verse from Isaiah. Rather than say the Spirit comes to rest on the promised Messiah, Cassian reads it as the Spirit shall fill him. So too for us, suggested Cassian, this breath, this Holy Spirit, is not a shield, but something that so penetrates us that it possesses us entirely. This breath of God fills us so completely that nothing else can disturb us, with a power so overwhelming it cannot be wrested from us.

We are promised that the Spirit of the Lord will rest upon the Messiah, who will be filled with wisdom and understanding. For ourselves, we hope that the breath of God, God's holy wind, will fill us as well. That we might find counsel and strength. That we might be able to breathe.

Meditation: How has the Holy Spirit filled you with wisdom and understanding? What is the Holy Spirit stirring up in you?

Prayer: Grant, O Lord, that we might be entirely possessed by your Holy Spirit. Breathe into us wisdom and understanding, counsel and strength. Stir up in us a passion for your justice, that we might bring peace to birth in our time.

Love's Long Feast

Readings: Isa 25:6-10a; Matt 15:29-37

Scripture:
The Lord God will wipe away
   the tears from all faces. (Isa 25:8b)

Reflection: There is such tenderness in the readings for today. I think of my mother, wiping the tears off the faces of my younger brothers, a cool cloth removing the last signs of pain and distress once the immediate damage had been dealt with.

I am struck in today's gospel by Jesus' tender care for those gathered. He is worried that they might faint from hunger if they aren't fed before he sends them on their way. The crowd, filled with those who had been cured and those who loved them enough to bring them before Jesus, might not have cared, thinking temporary hunger unimportant in the face of what had been done for them. But I hear in Jesus' concern God's desire to make us not just whole, but to see that we are replete, utterly enfolded in God's love, brought fully to life.

It is hard to measure the depths of this love God has for us. Isaiah tried, summoning images of a rich feast, with fine wines. The psalmist evokes an overflowing table and aromatic oils. I struggle, as I stand before the altar, God's very

Body and Blood held out to me, to see the full measure of mercy offered not just in some unknown future, but now.

The Talmud speaks of the wine saved since creation to be served to the righteous at the final banquet. But I realize we are offered to drink of what has been saved since creation every day in every glass of water we drink. Most of the atoms in that water came into being a scant second after the birth of the universe, dispersed through the universe to land here, for us. In much the same way, God's tender mercy surrounds us at every moment, we have only to take and drink of what has been prepared for us.

Meditation: Look up into the heavens and out into the immensity of the universe, or deep into a cup of water, where the atoms number more than the stars in our galaxy, and consider God's infinite mercy. What images evoke for you the depth and breadth of God's tender concern for us?

Prayer: From the beginning of time, O Lord, you spread a banquet before us. Enfold us in your mercy, and wipe the tears from our eyes, that we might at last see your face.

December 3: Saint Francis Xavier, Priest

Anchored in Trust

Readings: Isa 26:1-6; Matt 7:21, 24-27

Scripture:
"A nation of firm purpose you keep in peace;
    in peace, for its trust in you." (Isa 26:2b-3)

Reflection: I had gone for a walk when the storm was a smudge on the horizon. By the time I reached the end of the path through the dunes to stand on a small spit of sand protruding into the North Sea, the wind had come up in earnest. The sand rippled like silk across the beach, shifting the coastline in front of my eyes. It was an incredible relief to get back to the rocky outcrop that anchored the town and to ground that did not shift under my feet and slither into my shoes.

Still, sand is just rock that has been worn away, that has surrendered to the forces that batter at it. Water and air. Heat and freezing cold. Light. Isaiah reminds us that the facades we have constructed, the refuges we have built with our hands and minds, are no true refuge. They cannot stand against the elemental forces the world hurls at them. All these will crumble in time.

So in what can we take refuge, where is the strong city that Isaiah promises to Judah? In his "Blessing for One Who is Exhausted," priest and poet John O'Donohue encourages us to take shelter within the warm stone of silence and let its peace claim us. We ought not to surrender to the winds of this world, to be shaped by whatever blows by. Instead we need to draw close to and take on the shape of what protects us.

It is not what we say nor what we hear, but what we do, says Jesus, that gives us shape, that fashions us into living stones. For we are the foundation of the city of God, called to be open to the just, a shelter for the poor and protection for those in peril from the world. For deep within the silence that has claimed us is God, who has heard our cries for peace and for justice. Our God, who hears the cry of the poor.

Meditation: What in you needs to be ground away so that it can be reshaped by drawing near to God? Where should you set your living stone? What is it supporting in the city of God?

Prayer: Open to us the gates of justice, O Lord. Show us how to become a shining city, a nation of firm purpose, a people of peace.

December 4: Friday of the First Week of Advent

Five Minutes' Peace

Readings: Isa 29:17-24; Matt 9:27-31

Scripture:
One thing I ask of the LORD;
  this I seek:
To dwell in the house of the LORD
  all the days of my life. (Ps 27:4a)

Reflection: When my kids were small, we read them a book called *Five Minutes' Peace*. In it, a mother elephant goes from room to room, seeking five minutes of peace. She's longing for a cup of coffee and a look at the paper, unperturbed by her three children. In the end she resigns herself to three minutes and forty-five seconds of quiet. There are days, so many days, in Advent when I find myself equally chased from place to place by the demands of the day. Days where even three minutes and forty-five seconds of peace would be grace.

What is it I long for? Like the psalmist, I yearn to dwell in the house of the Lord, if not for all my days, at least for a few minutes. All too often I give up and let myself be dragged under by the torrents of mad-crazy-busyness that is the end of the year, crying out to the Son of David to have pity on me like the two blind men in today's reading from Matthew's gospel.

I find myself wondering if I walked out of my office today to find Jesus standing in the hallway, asking "Do you believe that I can do this?" what I would say. Do I really believe that if I ask, God will grant me five minutes' peace—or more?

I may have only a fraction of the faith of the two blind men, but perhaps like the tired mother elephant, I can be persistent in my pursuit of peace. If not five minutes, then three. If not today, tomorrow. I can pray for the grace to relentlessly seek God, that I might dwell within his walls, in peace all my days and beyond.

Meditation: In a colorful Advent drawing, Brother Mickey McGrath, OSFS, prayed that God might live in our hearts. Alongside, he suggested finding fifteen minutes each day to sit down with God and perhaps a cup of coffee. Spend the time thinking not of the demands of the day but rather contemplate all for which you are grateful to God.

Prayer: Come to us, O Lord, and clothe us in your peace. Grant that we might dwell with you in tranquility, eased of our daily concerns and healed of our wounds, now and forever.

December 5: Saturday of the First Week of Advent

Christ before Me

Readings: Isa 30:19-21, 23-26; Matt 9:35–10:1, 5a, 6-8

Scripture:
[F]rom behind, a voice shall sound in your ears:
  "This is the way; walk in it . . ." (Isa 30:21)

Reflection: No longer shall God be hidden, promises Isaiah. From behind, you will hear the Lord, to your right and to your left, his voice shall rise. I hear echoes in Isaiah of the last few lines of the prayer attributed to St. Patrick: "Christ before me, . . . Christ beneath me, . . . Christ on my right, Christ on my left . . ." Christ with me, always.

There is a famous chemistry problem that asks students to estimate the possibility that the next breath they take contains a molecule of oxygen once exhaled by some historical figure. As it turns out, in every breath we take there is likely to be at least one molecule that Jesus breathed. Oxygen works its way into plants and animals, into the water we drink, and the very stones under our feet. When Christ became incarnate, something of Christ started to find its way into the material universe in a new way. Christ has touched every stone that paves my path and that shelters me from the storms. Christ's breath stirs in the wind that blows past my face. In every breath I take, in every cell of my being, a bit of Christ's physical body resides. So, too, is Christ in each and every person I encounter. There are no unsacred places, said poet Wendell Berry. It's all sacred, all touched by God who came to earth to redeem us. God made flesh in time becomes God in all things.

It's a staggering reality. One that in truth I can hardly bear to think about: Christ within me, always.

Meditation: Look around. Where do you see Christ above you? Beneath your feet? Behind and next to you? Can you see Christ in the eyes of your neighbor? Perhaps more importantly, can your neighbor see Christ in your eyes?

Prayer: Christ, you promised to go before us always. Be beneath us, to hold us up. Above us, to remind us of our destiny. Beside us, to remind us that we are never alone.

SECOND WEEK OF ADVENT

Here Is Your God!

Readings: Isa 40:1-5, 9-11; 2 Pet 3:8-14; Mark 1:1-8

Scripture:
[S]ay to the cities of Judah:
  Here is your God! (Isa 40:9b)

Reflection: The ways of this life can be rough. We walk narrow paths, we struggle up mountains, we stand at the edge of terrain we cannot imagine ever traversing safely. It can be hard to hope that we will come across safe, hard to persevere, hard to wait for an end we cannot truly see coming. Yet we walk in hope. How? Fear not, cries Isaiah, look, here is your God. God, whose strong arm can sweep away any difficulty yet whose tender hands would carry us close to his heart.

There is a strength in God's tenderness toward us, one that says, "I can hold you up, no matter what; I can forgive you, no matter what; I am unafraid to face this with you, no matter what . . ." For the God who can fill in valleys and level mountains with a glance, who will dissolve the elements in fire and catch the stars up with a mighty roar, is one who can walk next to us, one we can lean against.

I wonder if I can enter into these Advent days brimming with the same hope that Isaiah can barely contain, a hope that dares to imagine the unimaginable. In his encyclical, *Spe Salvi*, Pope Benedict XVI expressed a similar worry. Have we "ceased to notice that we possess the hope that ensues from a real encounter with this God?" he asks. I know the lines of the story of our salvation so well—Christ is born, preaches, suffers, dies, and rises from the dead—that it's hard to grasp the staggering inconceivability of it all. Yet, here is our God. Here is our hope.

Meditation: Psalm 43 has the line, "Send your light and your fidelity, / that they may be my guide." What ways are rough in your life at this moment? Where do you need God's tender strength? Can you see where God has set a light to guide you?

Prayer: Gracious and all-powerful God, we place our hope in you. Kindle a light to lead us on the way, be near to us on the rugged paths, and hold us up when we falter.

Holy Madness

Readings: Isa 35:1-10; Luke 5:17-26

Scripture:
When Jesus saw their faith, he said, "As for you, your sins
   are forgiven." (Luke 5:20)

Reflection: We will do crazy things when we are madly in
love. Last summer, I had been traveling for work for several
weeks and was at last on my way to meet my husband and
my oldest son. Making connections in London, I found my
gate and looked for a seat. There was one, next to a gentleman
with gray hair and a lovely smile. My husband of a quarter
century and his luggage had rearranged his flights and taken
several trains and the subway across London to meet me, so
he could see me three hours sooner. Crazy!

   Whenever I hear this gospel of the paralyzed man and the
friends who carry him to see Jesus, I wonder what would
drive me to climb on a roof and try to lower someone on a
stretcher through it. Clearly, I would for my husband or my
sons or my siblings. But would I dare so much for a friend?
For a stranger? I wonder, too, about the owner of the house
who invited Jesus in and ended up with a hole in his roof.
Could he have imagined that anyone would take his house
apart in order to get to Jesus? The onlookers can't believe

either what they are seeing or what they are hearing. The whole scene seems wild, almost mad.

Pope St. John XXIII once suggested that without some holy madness the Church cannot grow. I suspect that without a touch of holy madness, or perhaps holy daring, we cannot grow in grace, either. The Gospel demands that we dare much. Dare to reach out to those the world rejects. Dare to forgive, each other and ourselves. Dare to expect forgiveness. Dare because we love God madly and God loves us beyond all reason.

Meditation: How much are you willing to risk to get close to Jesus? Who would you dare to help? To forgive? What holy mad thing would you dare with God's help?

Prayer: You love us abundantly, O Lord. Give us the courage and the strength to dare to be bearers of the holy for each other.

The Immaculate Conception of the Blessed Virgin Mary

Living on Surprise

Readings: Gen 3:9-15, 20; Eph 1:3-6, 11-12; Luke 1:26-38

Scripture:
"Hail, full of grace! The Lord is with you." (Luke 1:28b)

Reflection: I have a weakness for fancy Advent calendars, the sort museums publish with artwork from their collection. My favorite is a fifteenth-century triptych, the Mérode Altarpiece, depicting today's gospel, the annunciation. Mary is curled up with a book in a sun-washed room, utterly serene, imagined by the artist in the moment just before she notices her angelic intruder and all her plans—for her day and for her life—were upended.

In her poem, "Expect Nothing," poet and novelist Alice Walker suggests we be empty of expectations and live solely, and sparingly, on surprise. Mary, I'm certain, had no expectations of playing such a pivotal role in our salvation, no need to be anything more than who she was, the daughter of Anna and Joachim. She was as open to a day spent like any other day as she was open to bearing the Messiah. She left space to be surprised by God.

Reflecting on hospitality and Christmas in the *Catholic Worker*, Dorothy Day reminded us to leave space to be surprised by God. It would be easy to remember to make room for God, she noted, if we saw people with glowing neon signs hovering over their heads: Christ here. Or if they were beautifully dressed and serene like Mary in the painting I so delight in. People would have fought to give Mary a place to stay if she'd appeared in Bethlehem wrapped in gold cloth with a crown of stars, suggested Day. But I noticed last week no one was falling over themselves to give money to the woman on the Broad Street train who said she was coming down from a heroin high and needed something to eat.

We ought to help those we encounter, says Dorothy Day, not out of Christian duty, or because we are reminded of Christ or in case they might be Christ in disguise. We ought to do it with joy and ease because, perhaps to our surprise, they are *all* of them Christ. Make room!

Meditation: How do you greet the unexpected? Do you run toward it with joy or duck quickly around the corner? Where is God seeking to surprise you today?

Prayer: Fill us with grace, O Lord. Give us the eyes to see you incarnate in everyone we meet that we might greet you with delight and with joy.

Surrender to the Vastness

Readings: Isa 40:25-31; Matt 11:28-30

Scripture:
So mighty is his power, so great his strength, that not one
  fails to answer. (Isa 40:26b; New Jerusalem Bible)

Reflection: In a manila folder on the shelf in my office is a
letter to my two sons and my husband to be opened after I
die. It contains suggestions for my funeral Mass. Today's
first reading from Isaiah is one of the readings I've asked for.
I love God's instruction to us to look up at the heavens that
we might grasp what power he commands, so great that
even the stars march around the sky at his word. I've spent
my life looking at what God has done in the created universe,
gazing up into the stars and plunging deep into the atom's
mysteries. I see a universe drawn out from a single point,
the energies God commanded in its creation so unimaginably
vast that almost fourteen billion years later entire galaxies
are still hurtling away from us at speeds faster than light. I
am in awe.

The *Spiritual Exercises* of St. Ignatius of Loyola end with
his "Contemplation on the Love of God." In it, Ignatius asks
the person making the *Exercises* to imagine standing before
God and all the saints. Number the ways in which God has
shown how beloved you are. Consider all of creation, the

redemption of humankind, and the unique gifts God has conferred on you. Then, Ignatius suggests, think what you might offer in return to the God you are so passionately in love with and who so fiercely loves you. He suspects that like Isaiah's stars, in the face of so powerful a love, one could not help but answer. To say, "Yes, I surrender myself entirely to your will, O God."

Meditation: Ask God for the grace to reveal to you the ways in which he has been at work in the world and in your life, and for the courage and strength to respond in love to these gifts. What would you offer to God? What makes you worry you could fail to answer to God's call?

Prayer: "Receive, O Lord, all my liberty; take my memory, my understanding and my entire will. Whatever I have or hold you have given me; I give it all back to you and surrender it wholly to be governed by your will. Give me only your love and your grace and I am rich enough and ask for nothing more" (*Suscipe* of St. Ignatius of Loyola).

December 10: Thursday of the Second Week of Advent

Rivers of Mercy

Readings: Isa 41:13-20; Matt 11:11-15

Scripture:
I will open up rivers on the bare heights,
   and fountains in the broad valleys . . . (Isa 41:18a)

Reflection: I have lived in Pennsylvania—William Penn's green and verdant woods—for almost forty years. Water is plentiful here; I worry more about whether my basement will flood in the next rainstorm than when the next rain will come. Yet I can't quite shake off the dry dust of my California youth, still pouring the dregs of my water glass onto the plants on the window ledge rather than down the drain. Each and every time I cross the Schuylkill River, which bounds Philadelphia on one side, I am stunned by the amount of water flowing beneath me, relentlessly, lavishly tumbling toward the sea. So much water that enough flows past every hour to give a glass of water to every living person on earth. There is no need to hoard it by the drop or even by the gallon. And there is another larger river on the other side of the city.

So I stare thirstily at the river and think of these passages in Isaiah, promising deserts that will not just bloom, but that water will course through, spilling over banks and fountaining from springs. So much life-giving water that it will take your breath away. Each drive over the concrete bridge is but a taste of what I can expect to see, of what we are promised in the new heavens and new earth. But such an abundance is more than a hope of what is to come—it is a reminder of the lavish mercy we are promised here and now. A full measure flowing past, always there for us, always enough and more for every person, in every hour of our lives.

Meditation: The first reading from Isaiah summons images of a desert transformed to plains blooming with flowers and wetlands rich with food, forests spreading where once was a desolate waste. What images from the created world speak to you of mercy and God's lavish care for us?

Prayer: Lead us to the fountains of mercy you have opened for us, O God. Quench our thirst from these life-giving waters, wash us clean of sin and error in the torrents of your love.

December 11: Friday of the Second Week of Advent

Pregnant with Christ

Readings: Isa 48:17-19; Matt 11:16-19

Scripture:
I, the LORD, your God,
      teach you what is for your good,
      and lead you on the way you should go. (Isa 48:17b)

Reflection: Today we are halfway through Advent, and like everything in my life during this season, it is going all too fast. I long to take my prayer and my tea to a sunlit corner and linger with God in the warmth. But this is not the life I live. My office is filled with papers to grade, my calendar crowded with review sessions and meetings. The grocery store is packed with people, dodging displays of holiday baking supplies and racks of last-minute stocking stuffers. The traffic around the mall is unspeakable. These are not moments I should think anyone would wish to linger in.

But Advent is not a season for lingering—it draws us out, propels us forward. It calls us not to sit and watch the world go by, but to live as if we are bringing something to birth within the world and within ourselves. And as with all births, to be ready without quite knowing when we will be brought to our knees in labor. In a homily for students at Georgetown, theologian Walter Burghardt, SJ, reminded them—and us—to be people of ceaseless hope, a people always living into tomorrow. We are asked in Advent not to simply endure the waiting, the frustrations, the difficulties. Instead, we are asked to live with and into all the possibilities the difficulties open up: "This very moment, with all its imperfection and frustration, *because* of its imperfection and frustration, is pregnant with possibilities, pregnant with the future, pregnant with Christ."

My body still remembers the bone-weariness of being pregnant, the all-encompassing work of laboring to bring my sons into the world, those frustrations and difficulties never overshadowing the hopes I cradled in my heart for them. So I should not expect in Advent to be other than weary and stretched to my limit, for in this moment, I, too, am pregnant with Christ.

Meditation: I will freely admit that I find it hard to see the possibility of the Divine in the holiday traffic, let alone find Christ coming to birth therein. What possibilities do you see in the challenges of this moment?

Prayer: Grant us eyes to see the possibilities in this Advent, O God, that we might see what is coming to birth in us. Keep our feet from faltering and show us the way to you.

December 12: Our Lady of Guadalupe

Am I Not Here?

Readings: Zech 2:14-17 or Rev 11:19a; 12:1-6a, 10ab; Luke 1:26-38 or Luke 1:39-47

Scripture:
A great sign appeared in the sky, a woman clothed with
the sun, with the moon under her feet, and on her head
a crown of twelve stars. (Rev 12:1)

Reflection: Today is the feast of Nuestra Señora de Guadalupe. I have a tiny terra-cotta reproduction of her on my desk,
given to me by a friend, her face touched so often that I can
no longer distinguish the Virgin's features. There are no gold
stars spangled over her robe, the rays that surround her are
the same dull red of the rest of the image. I only know she
stands upon a crescent moon because I know the original
image. But as soon as I set her back into her place and turn
back to my work, the miracle occurs. I see her in my mind's
eye as the woman clothed in the sun in Revelation, crowned
with the stars, enthroned on the moon.

Mary labored to bring God into this world, clothed not in
gold nor standing on a celestial perch, but wrapped in the
same plain flesh all of us wear, bedded down on straw. As I
struggle in my own daily labors, to get the beds made, to
grade papers, I hear the words that Our Lady spoke to
St. Juan Diego Cuauhtlatoatzin when she appeared to him

on Tepayac Hill: "*¿No estoy yo aquí que soy tu madre?*" Am I not here, your mother, who you can always ask for help?

I remember sitting at the kitchen table doing my homework while my own mother labored to feed the family, peeling potatoes, and snapping the ends off the string beans. Her ears open to hear when I needed a small miracle to find the error in my algebra. The miracle at Guadalupe reminds me that Mary labors to bring Christ to us even now, that her ears are always open to hear what we might need, and yet cannot find the words to ask her son. Like Juan Diego, I can get so busy doing what must be done that I forget to reach out to God for aid and comfort. Mary, through this vision at Guadalupe, reminds me to reach out. And if I can't find the words to speak to God, is Nuestra Señora, our mother, not there to help?

Meditation: Where are you struggling to find God in your labors? What help might you need from Mary's son? Ask her for help in finding the words to ask God for help, ask her to show you Christ coming to birth in your daily work.

Prayer: Nuestra Señora, we are struggling with so many difficulties in our lives, with our illnesses and our anxieties. Bring us to your son, that he might comfort us, binding our wounds and easing our hearts. *¡Ayúdanos, Madre de Dios!*

THIRD WEEK OF ADVENT

Not Yet

Readings: Isa 61:1-2a, 10-11; 1 Thess 5:16-24; John 1:6-8, 19-28

Scripture:
And this is the testimony of John. When the Jews from
Jerusalem sent priests and Levites to him to ask him,
"Who are you?" he admitted . . . "I am not the Christ."
(John 1:19, 20b)

Reflection: Not me, said John. Not yet, he said. Keep looking,
for God is in your midst at this very moment.

Not yet, and yet. Advent is all about "not yet" and "yet."
It's not yet Christmas, a day I long for, when the light streams
in the back windows, illuminating the whole space. When
the house is quiet and I rest with my prayers cupped between
my hands, rising like incense with the steam from my tea.
And yet it has been Christmas, and God has come in the
flesh. He walks among us even now, should I have the courage to seek him out.

Meister Eckhart, a fourteenth-century Dominican preacher
and mystic, when asked why people can be reluctant to seek
God, replied that when someone is looking for something,
and finds not a trace of it, they become discouraged and keep
to the hunt with reluctance. If they find a trace of it, they will
take up the search with renewed energy. To gladly seek God,
one must first taste the sweetness of the Divine. I do not yet

come face-to-face with God. Yet I seek God's face because I have caught a glimpse. Not yet. And yet.

Voices in the wilderness of the world cry out our need for God. The kingdom we long for is not yet here. And yet. I walk past a man huddled on the steps of a shop in the city. In the dark before the dawn, I hold open the door of the shelter for a mother scrambling to get to work. I watch the bent woman in a long line waiting to board a train play peek-a-boo with a baby, buying a weary father a few minutes of peace. In each moment, should I care to look, I catch glimpses of God's presence. Not yet, they say, and yet, here I am, will you make straight my path?

Meditation: The Star Prophecy in the book of Numbers (Num 24:17) begins with the line, "I see him, though not now; I observe him, though not near." Where do you catch glimpses of God, here and yet not here? What voices do you hear crying out in the wilderness, asking you to make straight a path for God?

Prayer: O God, we are the people who long to see your face. Grant us the courage to search for you among us now and the strength to make straight your path.

December 14:
Saint John of the Cross, Priest and Doctor of the Church

Things Unseen

Readings: Num 24:2-7, 15-17a; Matt 21:23-27

Scripture:
[O]ne who sees what the Almighty sees,
    enraptured, and with eyes unveiled . . . (Num 24:16b)

Reflection: Today is the feast of St. John of the Cross. A man who was enraptured by the Almighty, drawn toward the one who is the light of the world, steeped in the psalms that were the backbone of his monastic life. He spent eight months imprisoned by his own monastic community, held in a space so dark he had to stand on a bench to catch the one beam of light that came through so he could see his prayer book. Deep in that darkness, he composed poems soaked in light and mystery and God.

I tend to put darkness opposite light, as something to be remedied by kindling lights literal or metaphorical. But John of the Cross did not see darkness solely as something to be vanquished, but rather as a place to meet God. Darkness drew him into the inexhaustible depths, a reminder that God was ultimately incomprehensible. One of John's "Sayings of Light and Love" advised against getting too caught up in what we can experience with our senses, in what we can see and hear and touch. We can become weighed down with the sensible, warned John, and lose the lightness of soul that eases our way toward the ineffable. Toward what is hidden from sight and unreachable in the mysterious depths.

This time of year, when everything from the pencil cup in the office to the street lamps on Lancaster Avenue are entangled with lights of every color that blink and dance, while bright Christmas music plays relentlessly in every shop, I sometimes think of John of the Cross's advice. Is all this keeping my soul anchored in the here and now? Are all these lights distracting me from the one Light that is, that was, and that will come? And I step out into the darkness.

Meditation: Go outside at sunset and look up at the sky, then turn around and look at the other side of the sky, where the darkness is slipping in. Look into the depths and let the weight of the world go.

Prayer: God of light and of darkness, turn our faces toward the depths. Help us to set aside our worries and distractions and draw us ever more deeply into the mystery of our redemption.

Quiet Messengers

Readings: Zeph 3:1-2, 9-13; Matt 21:28-32

Scripture:
Look to him that you may be radiant with joy,
    and your faces may not blush with shame. (Ps 34:6)

Reflection: Like the city in Zephaniah's prophecy, the times Alfred Delp, SJ, was living in were desolate and cruel. Despite this, despite his hands bound before him day and night in a Nazi prison, Delp wrote in his Advent reflections of herald angels. Not the triumphant angels who would ring out *"Gloria in excelsis deo"* on a Christmas night, but the quiet, inconspicuous messengers of God who even now walk the earth. The ones who are holding out a light in the darkness for those who have lost their way, the ones speaking a word of encouragement to people whose spirits are flagging, and the ones proclaiming that nothing, no matter how troubling, cannot be reclaimed and reborn in God.

In the first of four reflections he wrote for that bleak Advent, Delp suggested we, too, should be on the lookout for these angels bearing messages of consolation. Keep your ears sharp for their soft footsteps, he encouraged. Keep your hearts open to the seeds they wish to sow in your heart. Delp asked us to go beyond praying for an awareness of such angels among us. He invited us to consider being such messengers of God's infinite grace and mercy ourselves, holding each other up when we might falter, reminding each other to wait in joyful hope. In dark times to be such heralds of light is no easy task.

The angels we are expecting at Christmas are in reality among us now, their faces radiant with joy. They scatter seeds into the silence that waits patiently on the resounding chorus of Christ's return in glory. God grant us the grace and strength to do the same.

Meditation: Are you a herald of God's infinite grace? Where can you sow seeds of hope? Where might you whisper a word of consolation? Where might you offer an arm to hold up someone whose strength is failing them?

Prayer: Grant us the courage, O Lord, to draw close to you, that we might be radiant with joy, shining messengers of your mercy in the dimness of the present world.

December 16: Wednesday of the Third Week of Advent

Deep in the Darkness

Readings: Isa 45:6c-8, 18, 21c-25; Luke 7:18b-23

Scripture:
I am the LORD, there is no other;
I form the light, and create the darkness. (Isa 45:6c-7a)

Reflection: The universe began with a bang, astrophysicists tell us. It's hard to wrap our minds around the immensity of that event, and I tend to imagine it as a loud clap of thunder and a burst of brilliant light, prompted as much by the opening to Genesis with its mighty wind sweeping over the abyss and God declaring, "Let there be light," as by Fr. George LeMaitre's big bang theory.

But whatever happened in that first moment, it was silent—there was nothing yet in which to propagate sound, a word spoken would be frozen in place. Even once there was mass in which a word could move, it was dark. Light could not escape that dense snarling ball of matter. All the mass of the universe contained in such a small space I could cup it in my hands. We read the traces of those first moments in the skies above us, we look to the heavens for signs.

John the Baptist sent his disciples to Jesus to ask if he was the one promised, the Messiah. Jesus sent them back, not with a yes or a no for his cousin, but with instructions to read the signs, to look around them and see what had been done.

Dare we ask such questions now, demanding of each other where we ought to look for Emmanuel, God-with-us? To whom would we send? The signs have not changed, Jesus tells us. Look where the sick are cared for, where those whose steps falter are helped to walk secure, and where the Good News is proclaimed to the poor. Look not to the heavens, but to the margins.

Meditation: Who in your life would you ask to point the way to God? What signs do you see that God is here with us now?

Prayer: Behold! The Lord who has crafted the universe in darkness, who let light loose with a word, walks among us. In him shall be our salvation and our hope of glory—there is no other.

December 17: Thursday of the Third Week of Advent

Gone before Us

Readings: Gen 49:2, 8-10; Matt 1:1-17

Scripture:
Of her was born Jesus who is called the Christ.
   (Matt 1:16b)

Reflection: Where do I fit into my family? Who came before me? Clearing out my parents' house this past spring I found fragments of my history. The baby book my grandmother had kept of my mother's first years, one bright blonde curl tucked inside. Snapshots of people I recognized and people no one did. My siblings and I recalled the stories of these people we knew only from photographs, wondering over the never-before-appreciated resemblances we bore to our great aunts and uncles, bewildered by unrecognized names scrawled in the margins of albums.

I listen to the long genealogy of Jesus with much the same sense of wonder and bewilderment. Here are Isaac, Ruth, and Manasseh, whose stories I know well. There is Joram, a name I first encountered in a beloved piece of fiction. And every year I wonder anew at who Zadok might have been, vow to look him up, and then in the press of final exams, never do. I think about Mattan—Jesus' great-grandfather. What stories were told to Jesus about him? Was he a carpenter? Did some of his tools still hang on the wall of Joseph's workshop? Jesus did not come as a bolt of lightning from a clear sky, but in his humanity, he fits into a family we know.

In Eucharistic Prayer I, we pray to remember all those who have gone before us in faith. Like Matthew's genealogy, that line in the prayer brings to my mind those who have gone before me, marked with the same sign of faith that was traced on my head at baptism. My friend Maryellen and my dad, both gone to God this past year; my mother; my first husband; my great-grandmother who fled famine to come alone to a new country and whose wedding ring I wear. I catch fleeting glimpses of their faces and I breathe a prayer for them, that they might be with the saints we call on as we stand before God on the altar. Remembering those I was so close to, I feel drawn into this communion of saints, drawn into an age-old family of faith.

Meditation: Look up one of the names in Matthew's genealogy that you don't recognize. Why do you imagine Matthew included that particular name? Take a moment today to pray for those in your family whose names have faded into the past.

Prayer: Son of David, yet born of the Father before all ages, remember us and all those who have gone before us who showed us the way to faith. May we find each other at the altars on high, praising you together with the communion of saints.

O Lord

Readings: Jer 23:5-8; Matt 1:18-25

Scripture:
[T]hey shall name him Emmanuel,
which means "God is with us." (Matt 1:23b)

Reflection: The O Antiphons, so familiar from their musical setting, "O Come, O Come Emmanuel," are said at Evening Prayer these last seven days of Advent. Each day has its proper antiphon, starting with a biblical title for Jesus. The one for today begins "O Adonai"—O Lord—and ends with a plea to come and save us.

Advent or not, that phrase or one like it is on my lips multiple times a day. Just now, the cat appeared at my study window, demanding to be rescued from the roof, and I sighed, "Oh, Lord." I turn onto the main road to find it backed up, and breathe, "Dear God." An exasperated and exasperating student taps at my door and I choke back an "Oh God." "Lord," I wail, when the phone rings the instant I pick up my pen to grade the stack of homework on my desk—the one I've been trying to tend to since nine this morning. I step outside to go home, look up at the fiery sky, and gasp, "Oh, my God."

I sound thoughtless, I know. And frankly I wonder if this is just a habit, my glib invocation of the Lord of the universe anytime I am startled or something doesn't go the way I wish. But just maybe, just sometimes, it is the sort of prayer that comes from deep within my soul, that acknowledges my dependence upon the Lord for the very breath I use to call his name. Could it be that I am struck nearly wordless by my Redeemer, so that I can say no more than *O God*, hoping God will know whether I'm in awe or in need of rescue? O God, I hope so.

Meditation: So many of our prayers begin "O Lord," but who do we imagine when we use that title? What are we expecting God to do for us when we call out to him?

Prayer: O Lord, God of justice, almighty and ever-living God, Emmanuel, God-with-us, hear us when we call upon your name. Come, and save us.

December 19: Saturday of the Third Week of Advent

Astonished

Readings: Judg 13:2-7, 24-25a; Luke 1:5-25

Scripture:
Then Zechariah said to the angel, "How shall I know
this?" (Luke 1:18a)

Reflection: Zechariah—confronted in a time of prayer by no
less than the angel Gabriel—remained doubtful of the power
of God to overturn his life. I'm old, he tells Gabriel, my wife
is old, we've come to terms with how things are. But the
angel will hear none of this and, taking Zechariah's voice
with him, departs to do his work.

So often in these stories of angelic visitations we hear the
question, "How will this work?" I wonder if when I pray, I
am like Zechariah, so busy telling God how I think this
should work (or can't work), that I miss the solution God is
presenting.

It is good to be reminded that since prayer is a dialogue
with God, such a conversation involves listening as much
as speaking. I wonder if that is why Gabriel silenced Zechariah for all those months before John the Baptist's birth. Not
as punishment for his lack of faith or as a sign of the awesome power God commands, but as a tool to help him stop
to listen and be delighted by what God was doing. Zechariah
was, after all, promised joy and gladness.

In a General Audience, Pope Francis once asked if we were willing to be astonished by God when we prayed? To pray to God, Pope Francis went on to remind us, is to do more than lifelessly parrot the words of a prayer. Prayer, whether in familiar words or simply gasps wrung from our depths, brings us to encounter the living God. Prayer is a surrender of our desires for particular outcomes, and that is precisely what must happen if we are to be surprised.

Meditation: Find a moment to let your voice go silent today, and simply listen to God. What surprises and delights you about this encounter?

Prayer: O God, grant that we might be still and quiet enough to hear you in the silence of our hearts. Give us the courage to surrender our expectations that we might be astonished and delighted at all you are doing in the universe.

FOURTH WEEK OF ADVENT

December 20: Fourth Sunday of Advent

A Midwife for the Holy

Readings: 2 Sam 7:1-5, 8b-12, 14a, 16; Rom 16:25-27; Luke 1:26-38

Scripture:
"The Holy Spirit will come upon you, and the power of the Most High will overshadow you. Therefore the child to be born will be called holy, the Son of God." (Luke 1:35b)

Reflection: Poet Daniel Ladinsky's poetic rewriting of St. John of the Cross's short Christmas poem always conjures up for me the image of Mary, swaying down the road, heavily pregnant with Jesus. "Weighed with the Word of God," John described her, "pregnant with the holy," says Ladinsky. I wonder what was on her mind, as the time neared for the birth promised her by Gabriel nine months before. Was she worried about who would be there for her as she labored, or even where she would give birth? Would there be a skilled midwife to hand, or would she have to make do?

In a way, we are all pregnant with the holy, carrying within us the Holy Spirit, charged by our baptism to bring God forth in our own times and places. Consider then that each person who comes down the road toward us is equally weighed down with God, with God's word who is eager to enter into the world. Can we be present to these births that are happening all around us? Or might we worry that we are not qualified, that we won't know what to do? That we would be too much in awe to reach out for the holy, struggling to be born?

The courage to see the holy among us, to recognize it as holy, to reach out toward it, and the strength to hold up the ones laboring to bring the sacred Word to birth here and now depends not on our own merits. Instead, we might gather our courage to ask the Holy Spirit to come upon us, that the power of the Most High might overshadow us. Perhaps, then, we might say with confidence: Behold, I am the servant of the Lord, a midwife to the holy.

Meditation: In his *Spiritual Exercises*, St. Ignatius of Loyola recommended praying with your imagination, placing yourself into the gospel scenes. Imagine encountering Mary on the road to Bethlehem, heavily pregnant. What would you say to her?

Prayer: Most Holy Spirit, come upon us and fill us with all that is holy. Give us the courage and the strength to bear the Word and to continue to bring it to birth in the world.

Crashing Joy

Readings: Song 2:8-14 or Zeph 3:14-18a; Luke 1:39-45

Scripture:
"[A]t the moment the sound of your greeting reached my ears, the infant in my womb leaped for joy." (Luke 1:44)

Reflection: Twenty-four years ago, I was standing in my parish church rehearsing the music for an upcoming Mass, eight months pregnant with my youngest son. The choir director went to move the grand piano into place and suddenly its top came down with a discordant crash. I didn't jump, but the babe within my womb did, his arms and legs flailing out in that classic newborn startle reflex. It made me viscerally aware that there was someone inside of me whose thoughts were not my thoughts.

I vividly recall that experience every time I hear the gospel story of Mary's visit to Elizabeth. It surfaces more than sweet memories of my son, each time it reminds me to contemplate who is moving within me now, whose thoughts are not my thoughts. How do I notice and respond to God dwelling within me?

The nineteenth-century French Catholic novelist Léon Bloy wrote that joy was the surest sign of the presence of God. Surely Elizabeth's experience of both her own joy and that of the infant John the Baptist was a sure sign that they were in God's presence. In his encyclical on love, *Deus Caritas Est*, Pope Benedict XVI reminded us that being Christian isn't a purely rational choice based on some ideal or ethical system, but an encounter with an event, a person; a meeting with God that decisively orients our life. Elizabeth and Mary's lives were profoundly reoriented by their joyful encounters with God.

How do we discern God's movements within us? How might we know we have encountered the Word among us? We might be alert to those moments of unbridled joy that arise in our hearts. For joy is the surest sign.

Meditation: The O Antiphon for today, the shortest day of the year, begins *O Oriens*—O Daypring. How is your life oriented to the dawning light? Look for the moments in your day where joy is breaking out, quietly, or in crashing chords.

Prayer: O Morning Star, keep us alert to the sure sign of your dawning in the world: joy. Lighten our burdened hearts, and orient our lives to the joy of the Gospel.

Magnification

Readings: 1 Sam 1:24-28; Luke 1:46-56

Scripture:
"My soul proclaims the greatness of the Lord . . ."
    (Luke 1:46b)

Reflection: *"Magnificat anima mea Dominum . . ."* begins the Latin translation of Mary's canticle. *My soul magnifies the Lord.* When I was a child, I was puzzled by this use of "magnify." Was Mary's soul a spiritual magnifying glass? How could you make God any bigger? It wasn't until many years later that I learned that magnify in this sense meant "glorify."

I can laugh at my younger self, but she wasn't completely off the mark. An unnamed desert solitary—one of those men and women who went out into the desert in the fourth century to be alone with God—once said that prayer is a monk's mirror. Prayer shows you where you stand before God. But these two prayers—the *Magnificat* and Hannah's song (1 Sam 2:1-10) upon which it draws—are also magnifying glasses, they sharpen my awareness of loss and privation and desperation. Every time I pray these canticles, I am brought to see those who suddenly find themselves hungry or out of work or driven from their homes. I am reminded to pray not just for, but with, the hungry and those who will encounter bitter loss today.

These canticles also make me alive to the joy that nonetheless permeates this broken world. We been rescued, filled with good things. When I was a young widow, tangled in grief, hungry for what I had lost, these women's songs reminded me that joy was possible again, if I could but see the world with God's eyes.

We speak of balance in our lives, though few of us would seek the balance of gift and loss that Hannah and Mary experienced, granted sons who they would painfully surrender to God. These women's songs remind me that we live balanced on an edge, that our lives can pivot in a moment, but through it all God looms large.

Meditation: We are each afflicted and comforted at different times and places in our lives. Where do you see joy refusing to be silenced? Where is affliction dispiriting you?

Prayer: We long to praise you, O Lord, in the company of the angels and saints. In times of trial and seasons of joy, may we remember you, too, knew grief and joy.

December 23: Wednesday of the Fourth Week of Advent

Mystery

Readings: Mal 3:1-4, 23-24; Luke 1:57-66

Scripture:
Then fear came upon all their neighbors, and all these
   matters were discussed throughout the hill country of
   Judea. (Luke 1:65)

Reflection: When I was in high school, my family traveled
to visit my grandfather in Mexico for Christmas. I still can't
believe my parents undertook this journey—packing six kids
into a Volkswagen bus that surely had less power than Mary
and Joseph's donkey and driving over the mountains from
Mexico City to Oaxaca. Wearied from our own journey, we
arrived just in time for the celebration of Las Posadas, re-
imagining Mary and Joseph's long walk and search for a
place to stay.

A crowd of children billowed after the altar boys and their
tall candles, escorting the statues of Mary and Joseph, swaying on the shoulders of their bearers. House after house
chased us away, but at last we reached the square where the
statues were placed by the crib and a piñata was hung for
the children. When the papier-mâché ball broke, scattering
candy everywhere, my glasses fell off in the resulting scrum.

My mother found me on the edge of the crowd, confused
in the darkness, unsure where my family was. Suddenly my

five-year-old brother Gene came bounding up crying, "I found the big prize!" Clutched in his hands were my silver-framed glasses, covered in fingerprints, a bit bent, but unbroken. It was a miracle.

For years, my mother and I would remember this minor miracle, the rescue of my almost unscathed glasses from under the feet of a hundred excited children. How did this happen? The mystery of it all kept us telling the story.

Like Zechariah and Elizabeth's neighbors, thrown off balance by events outside the course of their usual experiences, we cannot stop telling the mysterious stories of Advent, trying to comprehend what has happened to us and why. The unending mystery draws us out of the everyday, luring us ever deeper into God's incomprehensible, luminous darkness.

Meditation: What small miracles have you noticed around you? How do they draw you closer into God's embrace?

Prayer: Overturn our expectations, O God, and let the small miracles you have offered us draw us deeper into the mystery of your being, until the day that we might see you face-to-face.

December 24: Thursday of the Fourth Week of Advent

A Tender Compassion

Readings: 2 Sam 7:1-5, 8b-12, 14a, 16; Luke 1:67-69

Scripture:
In the tender compassion of our God
    the dawn from on high shall break upon us,
    to shine on those who dwell in darkness and the
        shadow of death,
    and to guide our feet into the way of peace.
    (Luke 1:78-79)

Reflection: I know these words by heart, I pray them each morning, momentarily joining in the church's unending hymn of praise, the Liturgy of the Hours. Sometimes I say them gathered in the chapel at my parish, sometimes while I stand in a dim kitchen waiting for the water to come to a boil for my tea. But no matter where, I am ever in awe of an all-powerful God so careful of his creations. Tenderness. Compassion. God has shown the strength of his arm, to be sure, but equally holds us with gentle hands.

So many of us are juggling the demands of work and house and family and church today. When I'm pressed for time, I get tempted to play what my students call "martyr poker." Yes, you have so much to do, but I can top that, look at *my* to-do list! Christmas carols notwithstanding, heavenly peace, let alone rest, feels like a stretch today. Can we be as tender and compassionate to each other as God is tender and compassionate toward us, even in the midst of our frantic preparations for tomorrow's solemn feast?

I imagine compassion as a drop of water that falls into a pond, tiny wavelets rippling out from the center. Each act of tenderness, each time we show compassion to those around us, stillness and grace radiate outward. In the parking lot at the grocery store? Let someone else take that spot. Hoping to leave work early? Take on a task so a coworker can leave.

As the last moments of Advent ebb with the light, let us be God's tender compassion shining on each other, radiating out, guiding us together in the way of peace.

Meditation: Be on the watch for the Virgin today, have an eye to all those bearing God within and a mind to offer them shelter and a tender compassion.

Prayer: In your compassion, all-merciful God, guide our feet in your way of peace. Help us to be tender toward each other, quick to share burdens and to be bearers of grace in the face of chaos.

SEASON OF CHRISTMAS

December 25: The Nativity of the Lord (Christmas)

A Torrent of Light

Readings:
VIGIL: Isa 62:1-5; Acts 13:16-17, 22-25; Matt 1:1-25 or 1:18-25
NIGHT: Isa 9:1-6; Titus 2:11-14; Luke 2:1-14
DAWN: Isa 62:11-12; Titus 3:4-7; Luke 2:15-20
DAY: Isa 52:7-10; Heb 1:1-6; John 1:1-18 or 1:1-5, 9-14

Scripture:
The angel of the Lord appeared to them and the glory of
the Lord shone around them. (Luke 2:9a)

Reflection: When my oldest son was very young, he sometimes asked me to sing "his name song" before he went to
sleep. He meant the Litany of the Saints where his baptismal
names—Michael and Joseph—are near the top of the list. As
much as he reveled in finding himself named in the chant, I
suspect he found its heartbeat-like cadence soothing. I, too,
find comfort in a litany's beat of call and response. *Mary,
mother of God, pray for us. St. Joseph, pray for us. Angels of God,
pray for us . . . .* I imagine it reminds me of hearing my
mother's heartbeat as a newborn, held close to her chest,
warm and safe in the midst of a cold and confusing world.
I am here, it said, where I have always been, since those first
moments you came into being within my womb.

Litanies let me enter the torrents, let me stand in never-
ending streams of mercy and join my voice with that heav-

enly chorus that announced the Savior's birth. They let me wrap words around what cannot be captured in one line, or even ten thousand. They remind me that I am held close by God, close enough to hear God's heartbeat, close enough for him to hear mine.

Fourth-century bishop and Father of the Church St. Methodius of Olympus, reflecting on the second chapter of Luke's gospel from which we read today, gifted us a litany of light for this birth. Hail Zion, shine Jerusalem, your light has come, cries Methodius. The Light eternal, the Light supreme, the Light immaterial, the Light which illumines the ages. A cascade of images, the glory of the Lord poured over us, surrounding us even now. Beating out what we cannot wrap our minds around, what is hidden within, an unspeakable mystery. Light from Light. Christ, God from very God.

Meditation: The reading from Isaiah prescribed for the Vigil begins, "For Zion's sake I will not be silent." The silence of Advent has been broken by the Word, now crying out among us. Find a moment outside of Mass today to listen to the Word: pick up one of the readings, perhaps one you did not hear, and savor the voice of God speaking to us anew.

Prayer: *O nata lux de lumine*, O Light born of Light, you have broken the silence and rescued us from sin and sorrow. Light enduring, Light eternal, Light that illumines the ages, shine on your people, now and forever.

December 26: Saint Stephen, the First Martyr

The Scandal of the Nativity

Readings: Acts 6:8-10; 7:54-59; Matt 10:17-22

Scripture:
"Behold, I see the heavens opened and the Son of Man
  standing at the right hand of God." (Acts 7:56b)

Reflection: The readings for the start of the Christmas octave take us straight from the warmth of the stable to a brutal martyrdom in the earliest days of the church. Luke's Acts of the Apostles show us the heavens opening before Stephen's eyes, not on angelic choruses, but to reveal Jesus, standing at the right hand of God. I feel a bit like those who debated Stephen—I cannot face what has happened. But I must.

What has changed as a result of this birth of God into time? God is with us. The heavens have been opened. The Son of Man stands at the right hand of the Father. The reign of God is present, now and forever. What must change in me as a result of this coming of the Lord?

I must change my focus, shifting it away from the figures frozen in a manger scene and toward the living Christ. In a Christmas homily, St. Óscar Romero, then archbishop of San Salvador, reminded us that if we want to find the infant Jesus now we should be looking for him among the hungry and homeless children, those who will sleep not wrapped in swaddling clothes in mangers, but in newspapers on doorsteps.

I must reconsider my options. The preferential option for the poor, suggested Romero, was more than an awareness of poverty, watched from the outside like a burning building, but a willingness to run into the fire, a willingness to do anything to rescue those inside, to rescue Christ who is there among them.

This is the scandal of the Nativity, this is the stumbling block I face, that God demands of me not merely adoration, but witness. Not merely awareness, but action. St. Stephen was called from his community along with six others to seek out and serve those in need. We, too, are called to walk from the crib into the world, carrying with us the Light to the nations and a willingness to get our hands burned caring for Christ dwelling in the most vulnerable among us.

Meditation: What disturbs you about the world right now? Where do you see the kingdom breaking out? Where do you see Christ in need? What is God calling you to witness in word and deed?

Prayer: Disturb us, O Lord. Sharpen our awareness of those who are hungry and cold, of those whose lives are wracked with pain and despair. Strengthen our hands and hearts that we might walk courageously into the fire of the world to serve the least among us.

December 27: The Holy Family of Jesus, Mary, and Joseph

An Offering

Readings: Gen 15:1-6; 21:1-3; Heb 11:8, 11-12, 17-19; Luke 2:22-40 or 2:22, 39-40

Scripture:
[T]hey took him up to Jerusalem to present him to the Lord
. . . and to offer the sacrifice of *a pair of turtledoves* . . .
(Luke 2:22b, 24a)

Reflection: Mary and Joseph took their infant son to the temple and offered what a couple of limited means could—not a lamb, but a pair of turtledoves. They placed him in the hands of Simeon, who had waited a lifetime to see the salvation God promised to Israel.

A quarter of a century ago, my husband and I bundled our firstborn son up and brought him to the doors of our parish church. What do you ask of the church? Baptism, we said. The congregation sang the Litany of the Saints over him, Fr. Adrian poured water over his head and anointed him with oil. We brought him home again, we had lunch, and put him in the arms of his grandmother, her sight already dimmed. It was all light and glory and grace.

It was an offering we made that day. We surrendered his life, submerging him in the waters of baptism to emerge a new creation, reborn a child of God, clothed in Christ. And bound to the mystery that is Christ's life: passion, death, and resurrection. Bound to the cross in all its anguish and equally its glory.

Each time I walk past the baptismal font, I think of Mike's baptism. I taste of the same cup that Mary and Joseph drank of and grasp a bit more deeply how unsparingly generous their assent to their angelic visitors was. They said "yes" to God, committing their own lives, but in doing so they unreservedly said "yes" for their son. Saying "yes" to offering up the one thing any parent knows matters more to you than your own life—your child's life. Binding us all into the mystery of the cross and the resurrection. That offering takes my breath away.

Meditation: Think about who has brought you to the practice of the faith, to baptism, whether as a child or as an adult. What did they offer up to do that? How have they modeled for you what it means to be clothed in Christ, bound to his cross, caught up in glory in his resurrection?

Prayer: We were clothed in Christ at our baptism, O Lord. Grant us the grace to continue to surrender our lives and all we hold dear to your will. Stand by us as we bear our crosses and welcome us into the glory of your kingdom.

Dark Times

Readings: 1 John 1:5–2:2; Matt 2:13-18

Scripture:
This is the message that we have heard from Jesus Christ
and proclaim to you: God is light, and in him there is no
darkness at all. (1 John 1:5)

Reflection: I read this morning in the newspaper of children,
infants and toddlers, ambushed on a dusty road. I could tell
you which road, but the dark truth is, I can say this on any
day: children died because they were a threat to power and
I read about it in the paper. Light threatens the darkness,
because evil and darkness know they cannot possibly win
out. I've read about it, today, in the Scriptures.

But the point John makes in his letter is precisely that this
battle between light and darkness is not just to be read about,
but must be engaged in. We must walk in the light, we must
carry the light into these dark corners of the world. I deceive
myself when I hold the darkness at arm's length, claiming I
am powerless to avert tragedy and ruin in places far away. I
delude myself if I imagine that the way I live my life in no
way contributes to ravaging the earth and diminishing the
dignity of those who dwell on it. Ironically, despite my desire
to say I am not complicit in sin, I cannot name myself a saint

either, for a saint would take a lamp and head straight toward the nearest pool of darkness.

Evelyn Underhill, an early twentieth-century English poet and novelist, had blunt advice. We are the light of the world, but only because we have been set aflame by the Light of the world. Once kindled, we must not be decorative lights, or lights that loiter about the edges, but useful lights. We must not be afraid to pick up our lamps and stride into the world, aglow with the glory of God, in search of those who yearn for light.

Meditation: Though confession feels like a Lenten practice, the practice of a general examination of conscience seems apt at the edge of the new year as we celebrate beginnings, secular and liturgical. Find a moment to sit with the world, and notice the particular ways your life casts shadows on others. Listen to where you are called to bring light into the darkness and comfort to those who are trapped within it.

Prayer: With your birth you pulled the world out of darkness, O Lord. Once more you breathed upon the chaos that we might have life and have it to the full. Light our lamps, that we might carry you into the dark and dispel the evils that dwell there.

December 29:
Fifth Day within the Octave of the Nativity of the Lord

How Do We Know Him?

Readings: 1 John 2:3-11; Luke 2:22-35

Scripture:
The way we may be sure that we know Jesus is to keep his
    commandments. (1 John 2:3)

Reflection: How did Simeon know Jesus was the baby he
was waiting for, the anointed of the Lord? How are we sure
that we are able to recognize Jesus? Each Christmas brings
me face-to-face with the reality of a God who has put himself
into our hands, a God revealed in the unassuming and the
everyday.

Christmas nudges me to look outside myself, to look
around the edges. God is not safely swaddled in a manger
waiting for me to come adore him, but God is huddling in
the icy rain on the corner of Lancaster and Morris, wishing
for dry shoes. God is peering at a phone, trying to find the
number for the local shelter so her children don't have to
sleep in the car again tonight. God is being mocked for being
gay, for being an immigrant, for being elderly.

Jesus handed himself over to others from the very start,
into Mary and Joseph's arms, and into Simeon's arms. Like
Simeon, we have been called to point out God here and now.
To say to each other, here is God shivering in the rain, here

is God hungry, here is God scorned. We are called to gather God into our arms. To say to those who are worn out with struggle, come in and sit down with us.

How can we be sure we've found the One who has brought salvation and light and glory to us all? John tells us in his letter: keep God's commandments. Walk just as Jesus walked. Love each other as we have been loved by God. Hold each other's needs as our own.

God has put himself into our hands, a Light for the nations, a Light for each other. Point him out. Embrace him. Love the Lord your God, and your neighbor as yourself.

Meditation: What gift of a need met can you give someone? Invite a lonely neighbor for a walk. Take dinner to the family with toddlers. Leave a few extra quarters by the dryers at the laundromat. Leave that parking spot close to the door for someone more in need.

Prayer: Jesus, you taught us that love was the greatest commandment. Reveal yourself to us in the poor and the stranger. Show us how to cherish our neighbors more dearly.

December 30:
Sixth Day within the Octave of the Nativity of the Lord

Let Flash to the Shire

Readings: 1 John 2:12-17; Luke 2:36-40

Scripture:
Tremble before him, all the earth.
Say among the nations: The LORD is king. (Ps 96:9b-10a)

Reflection: The entrance antiphon for today takes its inspiration from the book of Wisdom: "[W]hen peaceful stillness encompassed everything / and the night in its swift course was half spent, / Your all-powerful word from heaven's royal throne / leapt into the . . . land" (18:14-15). What has leapt from the stillness and the silence to us? The prophetess Anna was willing to tell all who would listen about this child who had come to redeem them. I wonder what words she used to describe the infant Jesus, and what she knew of his destiny. Luke says only that she gave thanks to God. The quote from Wisdom brings to mind Gerard Manley Hopkins SJ's epic poem "The Wreck of the Deutschland," with its description of Christ-come-to-earth. Hopkins calls this infant heaven-flung and heart-fleshed, God come forth from the thunder-throne, a dayspring in our dimness, a crimson-kissed Light rising in the east.

I wonder if Anna would have used similar images to Hopkins, pulled from the psalms or the book of Wisdom, to help her listeners see beyond the infant in arms—wrinkled, tiny, helpless—to the all-powerful God now manifest. Can we see both the delightful babe and the thundering God before whom we tremble? Can we see that our God comes in strength, not to dazzle us, not in search of praise, but desiring to bowl us over with joy? God does not hurl bolts of lightning our way, but offers his strong arm to lean on, a shower of light to dawn on us. He makes the world firm, he governs us with equity. He burns so brightly we cannot mistake him for anything other than Light from Light, God from God. He burns so brightly that we cannot lose our way.

Meditation: Take a few moments to pray with these images of an earth resounding to God come from his throne. Read Psalm 97, where God's lightnings illuminate the world, or Psalm 96 where the earth trembles, or find a copy of Hopkins's "The Wreck of the Deutschland."

Prayer: You are a Light to the nations, O Lord, and from your fullness we have received grace upon grace. Keep our eyes on your dawning Light that we might never lose our way.

December 31:
Seventh Day within the Octave of the Nativity of the Lord

Written in Light

Readings: 1 John 2:18-21; John 1:1-18

Scripture:
In the beginning was the Word,
    and the Word was with God,
    and the Word was God. (John 1:1)

Reflection: In his *City of God*, St. Augustine recounts a story he heard from St. Simplicianus, a late fourth-century bishop of Milan. Simplicianus recalled a pagan scholar telling him that the opening lines to John's gospel "should be written in letters of gold and hung up in all the churches in the most conspicuous place." This is where our faith begins. In the darkness, yearning for light, life, and God to come among us. We look for a word, we look for the Word.

As a chemist, light is part of my toolkit. Chemists see light as active. It doesn't just illuminate what is there, temporarily driving away the darkness—it can fundamentally change what it touches. One molecule becomes another, matter is transformed. Even more wonderfully, once the light has soaked into a molecule, light can shine forth again, in new ways and new directions.

The Light has shone on us in the darkness, and we have been fundamentally changed. We have become children of

God. What's more, we are called to not just reflect this divine Light, but to be ablaze with it ourselves. We are the light of the world. We have been kindled, we hear in St. Matthew's gospel, not to be hidden under a bowl, or within the walls of our parish churches, but to shine forth, banishing the darkness around us.

In these deep winter days, I imagine John's words, written in letters of gold, shimmering on the walls of churches everywhere, catching the light and reflecting it back to us. Reminding us that the Word became flesh and made his dwelling among us, and we saw his glory, saw him full of grace and truth. I look for the Light dwelling among us, praying that it might change me, that I, too, might be aflame with the Word and filled with grace.

Meditation: What words from the Scriptures would you write in gold and hang on walls for all to see? How have and how could these words fundamentally transform you?

Prayer: God from God, Word-made-flesh, all things begin in you, all things end in you. May we be transformed by the light that dawned at your birth. May we be aflame with the Gospel and filled with grace.

Ever Blessing

Readings: Num 6:22-27; Gal 4:4-7; Luke 2:16-21

Scripture:
"So shall they invoke my name upon the Israelites, and I
   will bless them." (Num 6:27)

Reflection: A Dominican sister once told me she taught her
young students that everyone can bless. I think of her advice
often and let it encourage me to bless the people, places, and
times I encounter. I blessed my children each night before
they slept, signing them with the cross on their foreheads
and the words, "May God and all his angels watch over
you." I bless my students' exams, that they might be free of
anxiety and full of wisdom. Poet and priest John O'Donohue
wrote that to bless is to invoke, to call forth. Blessings are
springboards for the Holy Spirit to sweep into a particular
moment, he noted.

   Blessings are about being present. They require our presence to each other and our attention to the circumstances of
each other's lives. We bless the newly born, the newly mar-
ried, the dying. We bless ourselves at meals. Equally, blessings remind us of God's presence to us, God's attention to
us in all the moments of our lives, ordinary and extraordinary. This is how you shall bless, God told Moses. With kind-

ness and peace. With presence: God's face shining upon us, God keeping us close and safe and whole.

To bless is to have hope, to have faith, to bear witness to someone and something beyond ourselves. Blessings call forth something of the divine in both the one blessing and the one who is blessed. Mary is both blessed and blessing. She is blessed, God intimately present to her. God within her. She blesses us, brings God's presence to us clothed in flesh. Through her, God is with us.

Meditation: Madeleine L'Engle wrote in her memoir, *A Stone for a Pillow,* that it is salutary to bless those we find difficult. She advised blessing without expectation, to rely on God to be present and active in the situation. L'Engle suggested blessing six people you don't like before breakfast each morning. Try quietly blessing one person or situation you find vexing today.

Prayer: May the Lord bless you and keep you. May the Lord's face shine upon you. May the Lord bring you and all those you love a profound and everlasting peace.

January 2: Saints Basil the Great and Gregory Nazianzen,
Bishops and Doctors of the Church

Who Are You?

Readings: 1 John 2:22-28; John 1:19-28

Scripture:
"I am *the voice of one crying out in the desert,*
'Make straight the way of the Lord,' . . ." (John 1:23)

Reflection: This gospel, with its cry to prepare the way for the Lord, always seems to me to belong to beginnings—the beginning of Lent, the beginning of Advent, the beginning of Jesus' public ministry. But here it is, in the middle of the Christmas season, after we have just spent weeks preparing to celebrate the mystery of the incarnation. We're in all likelihood exhausted from all the preparing of music and liturgies and holiday meals. I'm certainly not ready to plunge back into the ordinary realities of life, and would rather ignore voices crying out briskly from the desert of winter, "straighten up, there is work to be done."

It is so tempting to sit just a while longer with an infant Jesus, quietly asleep in a manger, but I sometimes worry if what is so appealing to me about Jesus as a baby is that he can't talk. Could I imagine instead sitting down across the table from Jesus as an adult? What would he ask me? How would I respond? Would I have the courage to listen, rather than speak? To hear the challenging as well as the consoling?

In the *Spiritual Exercises*, St. Ignatius of Loyola recommends these sorts of prayerful conversations with God. Talk to Jesus, Ignatius urges, as you might to a friend. Feel free to use your imagination to set the stage for your meeting. Take your cues from the Renaissance painters—or David Wilkie who draws the incisive *Coffee with Jesus* strip, where characters meet Jesus dressed in a suit and tie over a hot beverage at the local coffee shop—and don't worry about getting the historical details correct. The point is to create a space to invite Jesus into your life as it is, here and now.

Perhaps it *is* time to tune into John the Baptist. Time to stop imagining falling on my knees in silent adoration when the angels sing and instead take my cup of tea, sit quietly down and talk to Jesus. To seek the advice of the one we call Wonder-Counselor and Prince of Peace. The Word made flesh who dwells among us.

Meditation: Dorothy Day often took her coffee outside in the morning to pray. Find a quiet moment today to have a cup of coffee—or tea—with Jesus and listen to what he has in mind for you.

Prayer: Jesus—truly God and truly human—come to us in the ordinary moments of our lives. Grant us the grace to hear what you have to say, that we might make a straight and level pathway for you in the world we live in.

EPIPHANY AND
BAPTISM OF THE LORD

January 3: The Epiphany of the Lord

The Art of Packing a Camel

Readings: Isa 60:1-6; Eph 3:2-3a, 5-6; Matt 2:1-12

Scripture:
Then they opened their treasures and offered him gifts of
gold, frankincense, and myrrh. (Matt 2:11b)

Reflection: My mental image of these wise visitors from the
East always includes their camels, though Matthew makes
no mention of their means of transportation. Still, thanks to
Isaiah, visions of kings pulling gifts from the backs of pre-
cariously packed camels dance in my head. A decade ago,
on the feast of the Epiphany, I began a thirty-day silent retreat. Deciding what to pack for this month apart drove me
to contemplate what the magi packed—beyond the gold,
frankincense, and myrrh—when what they carried could be
a matter of life and death. Where you might have to sit on
what you packed, feeling all the lumps and odd edges of
your baggage. And where balance was not a metaphor, but
a hard reality.

In his opera, *Amahl and the Night Visitors,* Gian Carlo Menotti
has King Kaspar packing a box for every eventuality, lapis
lazuli against malaria and jasper to find water. Packing for
this time away, I was tempted by my own version of Kaspar's
"just-in-case" box. Should I tuck in a few bags of chamomile
tea just in case I might want a soothing cup one afternoon?

Aspirin in case I got a headache? They were small, they wouldn't take up much room.

And then I worried that if I cushioned myself so well against the lumps and edges of this retreat, I wasn't leaving room for God to get in. I didn't want to be so prepared that my fundamental dependence on God for my every breath was obscured by tea bags and aspirin. Such small things that were suddenly taking up too much room.

I think of those camels now when I pack my bag for work, trying to strike a balance between space for what I need—my lunch—and space for God, which I need as much as my lunch.

Meditation: St. Gregory the Great spoke of the three gifts of the magi as symbols of the gifts we need for our journey of faith. Gold is wisdom; incense, prayer; and myrrh, self-denial. Where are you tucking wisdom, prayer, and self-denial into your day?

Prayer: God, grant us the wisdom to leave room for you to work in our lives. Keep us faithful in prayer and strengthen us in our self-denial.

January 4: Saint Elizabeth Ann Seton, Religious

The Kingdom Is Real

Readings: 1 John 3:22–4:6; Matt 4:12-17, 23-25

Scripture:
From that time on, Jesus began to preach and say, "Repent, for the Kingdom of heaven is at hand." (Matt 4:17)

Reflection: I first learned of the Trappist monks of the monastery Notre-Dame de l'Atlas in Tibhirine in a scaldingly luminous poem on the contemplative life by Marilyn Nelson. The prior of the community, Christian de Chergé, knowing he was at risk of dying at the hands of insurgents but unwilling to barricade the monastic community within their walls or flee, wrote a letter in which he forgave his murderer. He wrote, too, of his own remorse for the ways in which he—and all of us—was an accomplice to the evil that yet marauds through the world. He hoped before his death for a moment of lucidity that would allow him to forgive and to beg forgiveness of his fellow human beings and of God. It is a powerful reminder that repentance is for us all, that we are all standing at the brink of the kingdom.

Jesus heard of John's arrest, and did not hide, or set up a stronghold, but strode into the synagogues and marketplaces to preach the Good News: the kingdom is here. To proclaim the Gospel is to risk all. To preach peace means to practice peace. Even in the face of violence. To preach repentance means to grasp that all of us are all sinners, all complicit in the sorrow and ruin of this world.

God is with us. Not as a child in a manger. Nor hidden under his mother's cloak fleeing to Egypt, or working unremarked in Nazareth. Now crowds gather, and he is known far and wide. We have watched and waited, rejoiced and adored. Now it is real. Now is the time to risk it all. For God is with us.

Meditation: Guy Consolmagno, SJ, the director of the Vatican Observatory, often urges scientists not to hide their faith away when they enter their laboratories. How is your faith explicitly or implicitly visible to those you encounter today?

Prayer: Your kingdom is at hand, O Lord. Help us to proclaim in our deeds the Gospel to all we meet, make us beacons of hope in a world yet ravaged by sin.

Enough

Readings: 1 John 4:7-10; Mark 6:34-44

Scripture:
[T]hey picked up twelve wicker baskets full of fragments
and what was left of the fish. (Mark 6:43)

Reflection: "Will we have enough?" My two sons and I were
looking at the makings for dinner piled in the cart. The house
was full, and getting fuller with each passing hour, as people
gathered for my father's funeral. My dad lived far outside
town—there would be no going back to pick up more chicken
or tortillas. It would have to be enough.

I hear in the gospel Jesus' real questions to the disciples:
Can you trust you have enough? Enough to do the work I've
asked you to do, enough to feed those who have come to
listen. Can you trust me to work with you, to not leave you
empty-handed in the face of profound need?

For St. John, it's not so much that we love, but that we
have been loved. Loved enough to wipe away all our sins.
Loved enough that no one need go hungry. We are so rich
in love that we need not mete it out, or hide it away, or
huddle in a corner with it, lest it run out. But like the disciples I often worry that I won't have enough to share. Will
the cans of tuna and the jars of jelly I leave in the food box
make any difference? So I particularly appreciate Jesuit saint

Claude La Colombière's prayer to the Sacred Heart, begging God to enkindle the flame of love that is Jesus within his own heart, to set him aflame with a love as strong as God's love for him. A love so strong I can trust it reaches all those around me in need.

Will I have enough? Always. Enough and more.

Meditation: What small thing in your life might you share, even though you think it will make no difference? Ask God to show you the ways in which your gift spills over, enough and more to meet a need.

Prayer: Open my eyes, Lord, to see that I have enough and more than enough. Open my hands, Lord, that I might generously give what I have and more. Open my heart, Lord, that your light may burst into flame within me.

January 6: Wednesday after Epiphany

All Will Be Well

Readings: 1 John 4:11-18; Mark 6:45-52

Scripture:
[A]t once he spoke with them, "Take courage, it is I, do not
be afraid!" (Mark 6:50b)

Reflection: Medieval mystic Julian of Norwich's most famous saying from her visions of Christ is perhaps "all shall
be well, and all shall be well, and all manner of things shall
be well." She heard Jesus comforting us all, reminding us
that sin ultimately will not prevail. All will indeed be well,
I am sure, but when my life is rocked, I find this assurance
just a bit trite. As if I shouldn't be worried, even if the circumstances are worrisome.

But it is still Julian I reach for in trying times—just not this
famous passage from her *Revelations of Divine Love*. I find my
consolation in Julian's vision where it speaks to today's gospel, to the disciples in a wind-lashed boat far from shore: "He
did not say 'You shall not be tempest-tossed, you shall not
be work-weary, you shall not be discomforted.' But he did
say, 'You shall not be overcome.'" When my life is tempest-
tossed, when I am weary and uncomfortable, these are the
words that give me courage. "Of course you are worried," I
hear God say. "It's terribly stormy. But I promise, you will
not be overcome."

I suspect the disciples, who surely had weather-wise fishermen among them, guessed this might be a difficult crossing when Jesus sent them out. Yet, after a long day, they set out obediently. Unlike the disciples, I sometimes balk at what God is asking of me. Looking ahead and realizing it will be a tough slog, I'm too often tempted to give up before I've begun. But here, too, I take courage from Julian's saying and from the disciples. Set out. Yes, the winds might be against me, the boat might seem ready to capsize, but if I keep a sharp lookout, I will see Jesus coming toward me over the water. I cannot be overcome.

Meditation: In this new year, what is God asking you to do that you might be reluctant to begin? Pray for the grace of trust, that, as Julian said, we might be strong in both weal and woe, in joy and in sorrow.

Prayer: You did not promise our lives would be without storms, Lord, but you did promise we shall not be overcome. Grant us the courage to stay the course when the wind is against us.

Fulfilled in Our Hearing

Readings: 1 John 4:19–5:4; Luke 4:14-22a

Scripture:
The Spirit of the Lord is upon me,
because he has anointed me
to bring glad tidings to the poor. (Luke 4:18a)

Reflection: There is a section of a homily by St. John Chrysostom on the Gospel of Matthew that is often summed up, "If you cannot find Christ in the beggar at the church door, you will not find Him in the chalice." In it, John, the fourth-century archbishop of what was then Constantinople, pleads with his listeners to care first for those in need—the hungry, the homeless, the imprisoned—and only then to see to the adornment of the church, to providing golden chalices and lamps hung from silver chains.

Luke's gospel today shows us Jesus standing in the synagogue in Nazareth, proclaiming Isaiah's glad tidings are fulfilled. My reaction to this gospel is always one of profound relief, the Lord has come to us. Now those bound will go free, the blind will see, and the lame will be healed. All will be well. The listeners in Nazareth were amazed by his words, and so am I.

But when I stop to think about how Jesus intends to see this promise fulfilled, not merely metaphorically, in that we are freed from our captivity to sin, not just in what awaits us in heaven or at the end of time, but literally, here and now, I'm taken aback. For I suspect we are as much the glad tidings Isaiah is prophesying as Jesus is. We are the ones Jesus is sending to free the captives, to feed the hungry, and clothe the naked, to see that those who need to be rescued are rescued. In Jesus, I am not to be relieved of these concerns, but entrusted with them.

Today we are the ones sent to proclaim liberty and free the oppressed. Do we amaze those who see us?

Meditation: What glad tidings are you bringing from the altar into the world? Who will be freed and from what captivity by the work you do?

Prayer: Grant that our lives might amaze, O Lord. Make us staunch advocates of the freedom you proclaimed in the synagogue in Nazareth and tirelessly work to bring your glad tidings to the poor.

On a Word

Readings: 1 John 5:5-13; Luke 5:12-16

Scripture:
He sends his command to earth;
   his word runs swiftly!
Thus he makes the snow like wool,
   and spreads the frost like ash . . . (Ps 147:15-16)

Reflection: Early on a winter morning, driving to a conference, I came to the top of a hill. Below me stretched out miles of yellow-green pastures, dusted with frost, mist twirling round the trees that dotted the horizon, like the breath of God alight in the rising sun. I thought of my favorite lines from Psalm 147: "Who can withstand his cold? / Yet when again he issues his command, it melts them; / he raises his winds and the waters flow" (v. 17b-18). When I pray this psalm, even in the midst of a hot summer day, I often contemplate what is frozen in the world, in my life, in my soul. Where the breath of God might—with a word—unstick the ice dam, letting the waters flow and do their work.

I hold my own breath sometimes, standing outside on a crystalline cold night where the wind is shivering in the oak tree. My ears are sharp, hoping to hear God stirring, struggling to hear the Holy Spirit breathing on the frozen waters of the world. "Lord, if you wish," I pray in the words of the man with leprosy, "I can be remade and redeemed with a word."

God does desire that we be revived, restored, and redeemed. We have only to look outside and see a frost-touched landscape, or look up to the stars that march at his command to know he can do it with a single breath. I listen to the leaves stirring and I hear the words of Jesus to the man with leprosy, "I do will it." *Fiat.* And just like that we are made clean by the Word.

Meditation: Where is your life stuck, frozen in the muddiness of this earth? Can you ask God if he is willing to breathe on the iciness and scatter it like ashes?

Prayer: Lord, if you wish, you can heal us of everything that ails us. Shower your grace upon us, scatter the chill frost in our hearts.

January 9: Saturday after Epiphany

Citizens of Two Cities

Readings: 1 John 5:14-21; John 3:22-30

Scripture:
"So this joy of mine has been made complete. He must increase; I must decrease." (John 3:29b-30)

Reflection: The Christmas season ends tomorrow, and Ordinary Times lands—where I live at least—on a day likely to be gray and cold and without noticeably more daylight than when the new year dawned. I will take down the Christmas decorations and tuck them safely into boxes for another year.

The new semester starts soon and I'm plunged back into my daily round. Teaching and grading. Cooking dinner and doing the laundry. The liturgies will shift, too. We will flip past opening prayers and prefaces that speak of prophecies fulfilled and of miraculous births, pointing our prayers now to the paschal mystery that orients and shapes our everyday lives. Once again I will hear the words of my favorite of the prefaces for Ordinary Time in which we are reminded that we live and move within God, our entire selves depend on God. The prayer goes on to direct our attention to our day-to-day experiences of God's care for us, even as we know that God has promised us a share in eternal life.

The words of this preface make it clear that when I lug a basket of laundry down to the basement, I am living and moving within God. That standing next to the copier as it chugs out a hundred copies of my syllabus for the spring semester, my being rests within God. That my ordinary days are in fact lived in an extraordinary way, within God's care, within God's very being. In its Pastoral Constitution on the Church in the Modern World, *Gaudium et Spes*, Vatican II reminded us that we are citizens of two cities. We live in the world, but we are nevertheless citizens of God's holy city. We must strive to keep a foot in both cities at all times. We are in serious error, said the council, if we think that our faith is something apart and separate from our daily lives, from the laundry and the dishes and the carpool. And so I pray to experience the daily effects of God's care, to know that every move I make within this world, within these ordinary days, is made within God.

Meditation: I am always tempted to breathe a sigh of relief on this return to Ordinary Time. To turn down the volume on my prayer in the wake of such an intense season and step into a holding pattern until Lent. What might you do to keep the flames that were lit in you during Advent and Christmas alive in these ordinary days?

Prayer: Increase in us, O God, as we move from this festive season of beginnings into the ordinary time of our lives. Keep our feet firmly planted both in this world and in the world to come.

Harried by the Spirit

Readings: Isa 55:1-11; 1 John 5:1-9; Mark 1:7-11

Scripture:
[M]y word shall not return to me void,
　　but shall do my will,
　　achieving the end for which I sent it. (Isa 55:11)

Reflection: I was walking on a beach last summer, and came upon a sign that said, "Stay off the dune. Nesting terns." I dutifully gave the dune what I thought was a wide berth. A nesting tern did not agree. She dove at me, sweeping so close I could feel the air beneath her wings, and hear them creak as she pulled up. She relentlessly harried me down the beach, until I could make my way up to the bluffs.

One of the panels in the apse of my parish church shows the scene described in today's gospel: Jesus standing in the Jordan, a white dove hovering just beneath a cloud through which the Father benevolently peers. I have always imagined the Spirit as a gentle dove, enfolding the world under protective wings, comforting us. But after my encounter with the tern, I wonder if I've missed the point. A mother protecting her nestlings is fierce. Fierce with those she worries are predators and fierce with her nestlings when it comes time for them to leave the nest.

We hear in Isaiah of God's word, sent forth. It will not return to God empty, but will do what God has sent it to accomplish. The Holy Spirit is our fierce protector, making sure that the seed sown is not carried off. Equally, the Spirit harries us to be sure that we leave the nest, to move beyond adoring the babe in the manger. The Spirit is relentless, ensuring that the Word becomes flesh within us, achieving the ends which God wills. Yet, the Spirit is not harsh, for in the very line that follows this reading Isaiah cries, "in joy you shall go forth, in peace you shall be brought home; mountains and hills shall break out in song before you, all trees of the field shall clap their hands."

On the first Sunday of Advent, we pleaded in the words of the prophet Isaiah that God might rend the heavens and come down. That God might work awesome deeds, things we dared not hope for. God has indeed torn open the heavens and worked awesome deeds. We are not alone. God is with us, God breathes within us, God shines within us, God sends us forth. We could not have dared to hope for more.

Meditation: The Word has been spoken, what has it brought to birth in you? How will you do God's will in the next days and weeks, in the ordinary moments of your life?

Prayer: May we go forth from this season in joy, O Lord. May we be led in peace. May we hear the mountains and hills break out in song and see the trees shiver with delight. May we know God is with us, now and forever. Amen.

References

Introduction
Pope Francis, General Audience (December 18, 2019), http://
www.vatican.va/content/francesco/en/audiences/2019
/documents/papa-francesco_20191218_udienza-generale
.html.

November 29: First Sunday of Advent
Mary Frances Coady, *With Bound Hands: A Jesuit in Nazi Germany;
The Life and Selected Prison Letters of Alfred Delp* (Chicago:
Jesuit Way, 2003), 130.
Alfred Delp, SJ and Thomas Merton, *Alfred Delp, S.J.: Prison
Writings* (Maryknoll, NY: Orbis Books, 2004), 15.

November 30: Feast of St. Andrew
Pope Francis, *Evangelii Gaudium* 120, http://www.vatican.va
/content/francesco/en/apost_exhortations/documents/papa
-francesco_esortazione-ap_20131124_evangelii-gaudium.html.

December 1: Tuesday of the First Week of Advent
Bert Ghezzi, *Voices of the Saints: A Year of Readings* (New York:
Doubleday, 2000), 356–57.
John Cassian and Boniface Ramsey, OP, *John Cassian: The Confer-
ences* (New York: Paulist Press, 1997), 420.

December 2: Wednesday of the First Week of Advent
Maurice Simon, trans., *Berakoth*, https://halakhah.com/berakoth
/berakoth_34.html#PARTb.

Michelle Francl, "A Brief History of Water," *Nature Chemistry* 8 (October 2016): 897–98.

December 3: Thursday of the First Week of Advent
John O'Donohue, *To Bless the Space Between Us: A Book of Blessings* (New York: Doubleday, 2008).

December 4: Friday of the First Week of Advent
Jill Murphy, *Five Minutes' Peace* (New York: Puffin Books, 1999).

December 5: Saturday of the First Week of Advent
Wendell Berry, "How to Be a Poet," in *New Collected Poems* (Berkeley, CA: Counterpoint, 2012), 354.

December 6: Second Sunday of Advent
Pope Benedict XVI, *Spe Salvi* 3, http://www.vatican.va/content /benedict-xvi/en/encyclicals/documents/hf_ben-xvi_enc _20071130_spe-salvi.html.

December 7: Monday of the Second Week of Advent
Micky O'Neill McGrath, OSFS, *Good Saint John XXIII* (Princeton, NJ: Clear Faith, 2014), 53.

December 8: Feast of the Immaculate Conception
Alice Walker, "Expect Nothing," in *Revolutionary Petunias* (San Diego: Harcourt, 1973), 30.
Dorothy Day, "Room for Christ," *The Catholic Worker* (December 1945): 2.

December 9: Wednesday of the Second Week of Advent
David L. Fleming, *Draw Me into Your Friendship: A Literal Translation and a Contemporary Reading of the Spiritual Exercises* (St. Louis, MO: Institute of Jesuit Sources, 1996), 175–81.

John A. Hardon, SJ, "The Divine Attributes Retreat," http://www.therealpresence.org/archives/God/God_041.htm.

December 11: Friday of the Second Week of Advent
Walter Burghardt, SJ, *Sir, We Would Like to See Jesus: Homilies from a Hilltop* (New York: Paulist Press, 1982), 140.

December 13: Third Sunday of Advent
Meister Eckhart and David O'Neal, *Meister Eckhart, from Whom God Hid Nothing: Sermons, Writings, and Sayings* (Boston: New Seeds, 2005), 4.

December 14: Monday of the Third Week of Advent
St. John of the Cross, "Sayings of Light and Love," *Drink from the Wadi Cherith*, https://thirdordercarmelite.wordpress.com/carmelite-feast-days/st-john-of-the-cross-priest-and-doctor/sayings-of-light-and-love-st-john-of-the-cross/.

December 15: Tuesday of the Third Week of Advent
Alfred Delp, SJ, and Thomas Merton, *Alfred Delp, S.J.: Prison Writings* (Maryknoll, NY: Orbis Books, 2004), 17–19.

December 19: Saturday of the Third Week of Advent
Pope Francis, General Audience (November 15, 2017), http://www.vatican.va/content/francesco/en/audiences/2017/documents/papa-francesco_20171115_udienza-generale.html.

December 20: Fourth Sunday of Advent
Daniel J. Ladinsky, "If You Want," in *Love Poems from God: Twelve Sacred Voices from the East and West* (New York: Penguin Compass, 2002), 306–7.

December 21: Monday of the Fourth Week of Advent
Pope Benedict XVI, *Deus Caritas Est* 3, http://www.vatican.va
/content/benedict-xvi/en/encyclicals/documents/hf_ben
-xvi_enc_20051225_deus-caritas-est.html.

December 25: The Nativity of the Lord
Methodius, *Oration on Simeon and Anna*, trans. William R. Clark,
from *Ante-Nicene Fathers*, vol. 6, ed. Alexander Roberts, James
Donaldson, and A. Cleveland Coxe (Buffalo, NY: Christian
Literature Publishing, 1886), revised and edited for New Advent by Kevin Knight, http://www.newadvent.org/fathers
/0627.htm.

December 26: Saint Stephen, the First Martyr
Óscar Romero, *The Scandal of Redemption: When God Liberates the
Poor, Saves Sinners, and Heals Nations*, ed. Carolyn Kurtz
(Walden, NY: Plough Publishing House, 2018), 27.

December 28: The Holy Innocents, Martyrs
Evelyn Underhill, *Light of Christ: Addresses given at the House of
Retreat Pleshey, in May, 1932* (Eugene, OR: Wipf and Stock,
2004), 41–42.

**December 30: Sixth Day within the Octave of the Nativity of
the Lord**
Gerard Manley Hopkins, SJ, *Mortal Beauty, God's Grace: Major
Poems and Spiritual Writings of Gerard Manley Hopkins* (New
York: Vintage, 2003), 20.
Augustine of Hippo, *City of God* 10.29.

January 1: Solemnity of Mary, Holy Mother of God
John O'Donohue, *To Bless the Space Between Us: A Book of Blessings* (New York: Doubleday, 2008).
Madeleine L'Engle, *A Stone for a Pillow* (Wheaton, IL: H. Shaw, 1986), 121.

January 2: St. Basil and St. Gregory Nazianzen
David J. Wilkie, *Coffee with Jesus* (Downers Grove, IL: InterVarsity Press, 2013).

January 3: The Epiphany of the Lord
Gian Carlo Menotti, *Amahl and the Night Visitors* (New York: G. Schirmer, 1951).
Gregory the Great, in *Matthew 1–13: Ancient Christian Commentary*, ed. Manlio Simonetti (Downers Grove, IL: InterVarsity Press Academic, 2001), 28.

January 4: Monday after Epiphany
Marilyn Nelson, "The Contemplative Life," in *Faster Than Light: New and Selected Poems, 1996–2011* (Baton Rouge: Louisiana State University Press, 2012), 154.
John W. Kiser, *The Monks of Tibhirine: Faith, Love, and Terror in Algeria* (New York: St. Martin's Griffin, 2003), 244–46.

January 5: Tuesday after Epiphany
Claude La Colombière, SJ, in *Hearts on Fire: Praying with Jesuits*, ed. Michael Harter, SJ (Chicago: Loyola Press, 2005), 95.

January 6: Wednesday after Epiphany
Julian of Norwich, *Revelations of Divine Love*, chap. 27, https://www.gutenberg.org/files/52958/52958-h/52958-h.htm.

January 7: Thursday after Epiphany
John Chrysostom, *Homily 50 on Matthew*, trans. George Prevost
and rev. M.B. Riddle, from *Nicene and Post-Nicene Fathers, First
Series*, vol. 10, ed. Philip Schaff (Buffalo, NY: Christian Literature Publishing, 1888), revised and edited for New Advent
by Kevin Knight, http://www.newadvent.org/fathers
/200150.htm.

January 9: Saturday after Epiphany
Second Vatican Council, Pastoral Constitution on the Church in
the Modern World (*Gaudium et Spes*) 43, in Austin Flannery,
ed., *Vatican Council II: Constitutions, Decrees, Declarations; The
Basic Sixteen Documents* (Collegeville, MN: Liturgical Press,
2014).